AN HONEST
CHRISTIAN
POET

AN HONEST
CHRISTIAN
POET

IN THE DEAD OF WINTER, I HAVE SEEN
A WONDROUS THING

CHUCK WORTHY

CITI OF
BOOKS

CITIOFBOOKS, INC.
3736 Eubank NE Suite A1
Albuquerque, NM 87111-3579
www.citiofbooks.com
Hotline: 1 (877) 389-2759
Fax: 1 (505) 930-7244

Ordering Information:

Quantity sales. Special discounts are available on quantity purchases by corporations, associations, and others. For details, contact the publisher at the address above.

Printed in the United States of America.

ISBN-13:   Softcover   979-8-89391-839-7

                eBook   979-8-89391-840-3

Library of Congress Control Number: 2025915981

Table of Contents

I'm dedicating this work to the two most important women in my life.

My wife, The Beautiful and Talented Linda Diane Worthy. My Wife, My Love, My Passion, and the inspiration for much of my poetry.

She is my Shield-Maiden and the Star-Queen of my Universe. She is the source of the very best in me and my love and gratitude for her are as immeasurable as the heavens.

My Mother Helen Athelia Shaw Worthy. My courage, strength, and ability to persist in difficult times are owed to my Mother. Thanks, Mom, I know you are with Christ in His Kingdom waiting for us.

Author's motto in life:

"How can science, astronomy, and astrophysics come together to create poetry of love and life and forever? Indeed, in the dead of winter, I have seen a wonderous thing…"

Words or phrases that the author lives by:

"Dig into it, don't run away and keep working the problem."

"I was deeply moved reading An Honest Christian Poet. I was drawn in by Chuck's unique, sometimes painfully raw, and often whimsical point of view, as well as how he wove in his fascinating biographical commentary. He expressed an extraordinary depth of feeling, of love, particularly toward his cherished wife, as well as the ugly realities of living through war, illness, and pain. He didn't shrink back from total honesty yet somehow; I was left recognizing his hope and faith through it all." Bonnie Foxley singer-songwriter, speaker, and author of The Wardrobe of Inner Beauty.

"One in a while in literature you might come across a gem that gives you insight to the writer and their walk through life. This is one of those pieces. The trials and victories, the hardships and triumphs. And if you read between the lines, you will find a man that has seen much and has so much more to tell. I highly recommend it."

Scott Burleigh

An Honest Christian Poet is such a quiet, beautiful book. The title really says it all—there's this sincerity in the poetry that feels rare and refreshing. It's deeply rooted in faith, but not in a preachy way—it's more like a personal conversation with God in the stillness of winter. Some of the poems are simple, others more layered, but all of them carry this gentle kind of hope. It's the kind of book you keep on the nightstand and return to when you need a little peace or perspective.

Grace Eliot

LOVE

Forever Story

Our forever story stretches long, rewards are great. Crystal Columns shine, show our fate. Glory story written for His, our sake, through ups and downs our reward is staked. The 13th Valley we've come through, but you were made for me and I for you. Though seasons like thunderstorms rumble through, you were made for me and I for you.

Author notes; 39 years with The Beautiful and Talented Linda Diane Worthy...

The Star-Queen Refulgent

The Star-Queen, refulgent in her glory
My love for her, is a tale of stories
Her eyes shine with glory, as does her soul
The Star-Queen, the one that my heart holds. A Pulsar-Quasar among the stars, I am Hers, though near or far

Author notes

For Linda Diane Worthy

We are, we were, we will be

We are, we were, we will be
Sitting atop White Alice
Sunset over Great Tanaga
We are, we were, we will be

Turn to the east
Great Sitka
Afire forever
We are, we were, we will be

Tundra Stompin Lake Betty
It's ours
all ours, alone
We are, we were, we will be

Orcas, eagles at play
Razor-Back looming
Glory all around
We are, we were, we will be

Criss Cross the country
See what is to see
Know we're bound together
We are, we were, we will be

Author notes

Just a short look back on my Life and Times with Linda Diane
Worthy.

It is night

It is night, and I stretch out my hand
You are my Love, my mate, and so I pray
That I will be better, in heart and in Love
That you will grow stronger in heart and in soul
The work of your hands will be as gold
That I will have no other, as I grow old

Author notes

Waking up late at night and gazing on my beautiful wife

Calabi Yau

If I could fly away, I would not To be free of you, I could not
You are like space and time because I see you only in part.
Calabi Yau.
Grand, beautiful and full of wonder, but seen only in part.
Calabi Yau.
Touching the surface, your smooth perfect skin I am filled with
wonder, but I see you only in part. Calabi Yau.
You reach for the stars and pull yourself up, but your strength
is seen only in part. Calabi Yau.
My glory, my lover, my life deep within, I can see you only in
part. Calabi Yau.
They think they know you and see your heart, but in truth
you're known only in part, Calabi Yau.
Always the greatest is seen just in part, and so it is with you,
Calabi Yau.
Wife, Lover, and my best friend, but that is only in part.
Protector, Confessor and Confidante
That's how you hold my heart.
Please hold me closely, plant me in your heart, I'll come to
know you, this is just the start. Calabi Yau.

Author notes

This one I find very "interesting". While something of a poet,
I'm also very technical and love science. Calabi Yau Spheres/
Spaces are Hidden Dimensions in space and time. Astrophysics
and String Theory models suggest that there are an infinite
number of dimensions, most of which we cannot observe.
Egad, how do you get a poem out of that???

What I Want

To awaken
To come to life
To live and be satisfied, and more

To revel in the heat of ecstasy
To move the earth with joy
This is what I want
This is what I have In you

Author notes

Another poem for The Beautiful and Talented Linda Diane Worthy.

Bonded

She sings of being bonded together, Forever
And I reflect on those I love
My God, and my wife
These two have saved my life
Kept me alive
Strengthened my grip
Kept me, from the flames

Dried all my tears, subdued my fears, of life
Of all I have known, these two remain

Bonded together, their vows are true
All of their promises will come true
Bonded together, for now and all time
He gave His life, and He, made her mine

Author life notes

Another poem for the Beautiful and Talented Linda Diane Worthy inspired by a Twila Paris song.

To Have You

To have you, is, to have... Heaven
You are the One and Only
My prize, passion and glory, how I long to touch you
To Love you and only you

I sit, and think of you
I bring you to mind and a flame erupts in my heart I burn with passion and my chest tightens
My breath comes in short sighs and my pulse quickens My mind is aflame thinking of you
Your image floats in my mind, fanning the flames And I am consumed

I want to touch you
To feel you
Touch your heart
Feel the softness of your perfect skin

You take hold of my mind and seduce my soul
You lead me through the portals of Love
Drowning me with heat, passion, desire
I am dizzy and collapse at your feel, begging for more

Oh, to have you, to have you...
Is to have Heaven

Author notes

A poem for The Beautiful and Talented Linda Diane Worthy.

In my mind

In my mind I have you, body and soul
You are the warm, sweet mist kissing my face, warming my soul
Swirling around my heart, making me dizzy with joy

I breath you in, and I live, I touch you, and am alive
My heart pounds and my chest tightens at the thought of you
Diana, goddess of Love
Keeper of my heart,
Lover, and love of my life

Author notes

Another one for the Beautiful and Talented Linda Diane Worthy

The Moon

Stood on the balcony, watching the moon
Heart bursting with joy knowing you see it too
Love overflowing at the thought of us two
All of our lives and all we can do
Love that He gave us let us renew
That one special place in my heart is for you

Author notes

This is a memory from years ago. I was in Mt View, CA and had just gotten back to the hotel. In that beautiful clear California sky the full moon was glorious and as I stood there watching my heart was bursting with love for Linda Diane Worthy.

Mi' Esposa

Mi' Esposa, a man once said
Mi' Esposa, my lover and friend
Mi' Esposa, my friend to the end
Mi' Esposa, let me love you again
Mi' Esposa, stay close to me
Mi' Esposa, God gave you to me

Author notes

Written of course for The Beautiful and Talented Linda Diane Worthy.

Fire

In you I'm on fire, and you are the wind
You are my passion, you are my friend
I need to love you because you are mine

It's like coming home, like Christmas time
The gifts that you give me inflame me again
Come let me love you, my passion, my friend
No other soul is mated to mine
Come let me love you, just one more time

Author notes

For my Life Long Love, The Beautiful and Talented Linda Diane
Worthy

The Star Queen

I watched as she remade herself
Devouring every big book on the shelf
Overtaking those that started ahead Left in her wake, angry
and sad
Grasping the stars, pulling herself up
A mind so expansive, no, not like us
The Star Queen reigning on my heart's throne
Forever she will call that place home

Author notes

In the early 90's The Beautiful and Talented Linda Diane
Worthy completely remade herself.

We Are One

We are Rainier, we are St Helens
Standing apart, but are one
Joined from the beginning
Always, always one

We are the earth, we are the moon
Flying through space, but are one
Joined from the time of creation
They are one, Always one

We are the sun, we are the earth

Though far apart
They are one
Always, always one
We, like them, are one

Time and space thought far apart
We did not know
They are one

All these things are one
You and I, are one

Author notes

For The Beautiful and Talented Linda Diane Worthy

The Star Queen

The Star Queen Serene on her throne
Her soul swirls round mine
A blending of spirits divine, merging till we are one
Passion outshines the sun

She is what is not seen
Calabi Yau manifolds
Gleaming with universe unseen
And yet, I see my Queen
The Star Queen
Serene on her throne

Author notes

For The Beautiful and Talented Linda Diane Worthy.

LIFE
Pain Suffering Joy Endurance

Life is like a River

Life is like a river, the goal to swim upstream

We thought it would be easy, but it's not what it seemed

Jumping in all was constricted, gasping, coughing comes the breath

Scraping, gouging cross the bottom no air here to catch a breath

Bleeding hands grabbed twig and Vine, finding purchase on a rock

Coughing, hacking out the weakness, take a moment taking stock

A sickly weak voice rises up, asking Hey Man What's The Point

Hold on tight strap in tight make your home this rock
But, life is like a river and the goal to swim upstream

Cast off from the resting place, fight, struggle but don't stop
Those things we want and what we need are way up there, unseen

And life is like a river and the goal to swim upstream

The Glory of What I have Seen

Grinding away on me becoming Me...
Loving The Glory of what I have seen
Active Volcano, Great Sitka, afire forever, gazing upon The
Wonder of Great Tanaga's slopes of wonder. Come, Rest atop
White Alice and see..
.

Razor Back at the Birthplace of The Winds
Razor Back, The Only One, those of the lower 48, are not...
.

Have you seen Shemya? No Don't Go there
Adakians only know why...
On Shemya live the lords that rule the sky
Come uninvited, and you may die...
Now another Frozen Land awaits
Newfoundland, come, see, and keep pace

Author notes

Fill your eyes with The Glory of Creation

Shoes Untied...

Toppling down the wooden stairs thinking oh crap, why didn't
I listen to the wiser one who said, you should tie your shoes my
son, I think you really should. Remember if you trip my son,
you're falling onto wood. So, as I fly and fly on down, knowing
I'll eat wood... I think, you should listen more you fool, yes you
really should....

Author notes

Just a little fun, inspired by the admonition of a Wise Man, Bill
McMonnies

Laniakea Unbound

Restless, gazing at mountain, at what I've found. Sun moon, sky, earth, Glories of Glories surround.

.

From farest heavens stretches to earth, Laniakea by Breadth and girth. In immeasurable heavens what is life worth. Hands, feet and mouth, all shackled to earth.

.

Immeasurable heavens not bound by the curse. Unbind me, us Lord come break the curse.

Author notes

Seek to become like the Heavens above, Free, Unbound, loosed to BE what we should be. What we were made to be.

Those That Would Be Free

Best learn from God to fight My Friends, to fight hard and last.

.

Tis no mistake, no personal thing that knife thrust in your back. There sails in another knife, what will you do with that? Turn to flee thus run away, no, no sense in that. Take up sword and helm and shield, let us now attack.

.

As we fight and hack and spit, we know this one thing, done we have what life demands of all who would be free. Climb the mountains of today while others surmount theirs. Theirs is higher and to those low, tis no matter for compare, in the end, My Dear Friend, we all will breathe Fresh Air.

Author notes

A bit of an expansion of a previously written Poem..

Undertows Got Ya

Playing, swimming round out there,
18, strong as the sun, no place I can't swim, no not one.
.

Puerto Rico swim team, strong swim long. Drowning impossible, Thanks Dad, Mom
.

Dive in go play, farther than friends, I'm the only one. Look up, you're a mile out son. Swim strong now, that's it son. No, no, no, not gaining ground, undertows got ya, you may drown...
.

Recall training, swim parallel till currents change, turn, stroke, stroke stroke back again
.

So strong, so tired, made it back to the shore. Cheated death, again, let the dice roll...

Author notes

Based on a near drowning event in my life.

PF Flyers

Run faster, jump higher, that's what they said and By Golly, that's what I did. Ran Faster than light, jumped like Superman, just like the add on the TV said.
Ripped up trees by the root, older sisters in fright did scoot. Roared like a giant jumping down from the roof...
The Sun fled away, Mr Moon pissed his pants, so mighty had become the one time ant.
What to do now with the world at my feet? Climb highest mountain, explore the Deep? Destroy all crime, make people free? Shhhhh, Mom just said, Go To Sleep.

Author notes

It just popped into my head...

Shore Of Hope

Seized again by swirling sea, perspective as Chu Lai... Turbulence as Khe Sanh. Drowning, now and once again in sweeping flood of "WHY".

.

Grasping strands of vapor, hope transforms into TET, being pierced through once again, needing to forget.

.

Cast up on shore of hope, strength about to die. Tsunami breaking right behind, Pyroclastic flow boiling in the sky.

.

Time Dilation stills the scene... see Shield-Maiden, Glorious One. See, armor come back to you, Steed of War anew.
He is well pleased with you Child, but you are not through.

.

A million, million years from now hear the song anew. The song of Shield-Maiden, Glorious One, and all that She did do...
Author notes

.

I'll consolidate my thoughts here. I've watched Linda Diane Worthy suffer from these horrific conditions for well over ten years. Rather than describe the conditions, I will say this.
Over time they will cause you to at times: question your faith in God
question your will and desire to live drown in depression and desperation be crushed in soul and spirit

.

TERMS Used;
Chu Lai
Base during the Viet Nam war.
My Father was stationed there and whatever happened
to him in combat caused him to sleep with a Kar-Bar for the rest of his life.

.
TET
The Tet Offensive was an all-out attack by North Vietnamese and Viet Cong troops against American, South Vietnamese, and Allied Forces. It encompassed all of South Vietnam.
The Americans that survived Tet were universally Never The Same.

.
Khe Sanh
American Base was surrounded, under siege, and shelled for five months

Strong Soul With a Limp

Opened the doors drown my soul, innocent instrument of death. Sent with kindest loving intent, sharp blade in my heart, how I wept. Key to open hurt locker of shame, see the child wailing, broken, bent Watch the soul, flicker and die, blow breath from Heaven sent. Smoldering candle was not snuffed out. Bruised reed given splint Walking strongly now through life, but my soul has a limp...

Author notes

You know how it is. Events in Childhood follow you through life.

A Mountain To Climb Over There

We must persist on this road though unfair, must press on, no, cannot despair. The problem, is the problem, thus it wears. Soul mind and body gasping air. We must push on though no air, we've a mountain to climb, over there..

Author notes

Once again, keep going no matter what.

Little Lite Shining

Your light still shines, though you are gone, sweet love gone out from us

.

You lived so well, like the Balls Bell, furry ball of love between us

.

So young you knew pain but overcame. Your courage a thing of light shining

.

Lived long and well, freedom your fortune from us

.

Daily roll in the grass, life was a blast, your loving instruction to us.

Author notes

Beloved Dolce lived a life of love.

Break Through

Up from the 13th Valley, I have sworn an oath. No longer will anything hinder my growth. Damn this, damn that, and damn that there too. No matter what the hell, this one must break through.

Author notes

Just a few thoughts on Pushing forward at all times. The 13th Valley is a reference to the hell of Viet Nam.

Come To Now

No apologies for my life, I am who I must be. Your life is over there, that's where you should be.

With Shield-Maiden at my side, been through the gates of hell. This is me and she is mine, perhaps this is farewell.

You're thinking as in times gone by, that is not today. Hurry, catch up, come to now, understand and see.

Out of the 13th Valley now with wisdom at our back. As said before, I'll not look back, I cannot give a damn.

Surmounting now peaks of today, Shield-Maiden with sword drawn. Come now to contend with us, friend you have been warned.

Author notes

Ever get to this point in your life? Writing this one was refreshing! In my poetry the terms Shield Maiden and Star Queen are monikers for my wife, The Beautiful and Talented Linda Diane Worthy. Still, there's always someone trying to burst your bubble.

That Afternoon

That afternoon
Wars started, fought, won
Floods arouse, destruction, rebuild
Youth married, children born, aged and then...
Moon landings, Mars, Jupiter captured
With arms outstretched, heights ascended
Supper time, sleep
Tomorrow is another day
I want ice cream...

Author notes

Remember back in age when an afternoon lasted years?

Real Fun Time

As children, there were worlds inside our heads. Cities, States, Nations, Beast of our creation. Sailing among stars, we ruled near and far. Skipping across seas being all we would be. Expansive, without end, our creations, real and other friends.

Now the world is small, the tiny screen fills all. For things foolish, real and fake we, our own souls forsake. Claiming many friends, not knowing most, yet loudly we boast. Let's return to those times, when alone was good and real friends fine.

Author notes

Social Media and Online Life now seem to be more like a Second Job...

To Say No...

Up, out from the 13th Valley, shackles, chains on my back. I could not give a damn, I would not look back.

Slog through deepest valley, sticky plants, clinging vines reach out. No, I cannot give a damn, the path is up and out.

Suffer in the desert, God will I get through? Come now, look at me My Son, see what I had to do.

Drop into warm ocean. My ancestral home, place of Old Dominion, seat of Powers Home. Now untangled from that pain, from here I'll not roam.

Author notes; Sometimes only painful times can teach us what we want and who we are only

Topsy, Tervy Toppled

Hear them roaring in their pain
Screaming now in agony
The world, Topsy, Tervy Toppled
Weebles more than wobbled
Ask them what torments them so...
See that it is nothing
Still they must scream, cry and shout
Though tis nothing it's about...

Author notes

We all remember way back when we were little kids. When our apple carts were so easy toppled...

Vipers of Family

From high Red Place arrived we here, grasping open air. Shining in our power, hovering in thin air. Expanding growth and power, our kingdom oh so fair.

.

Dead place leapt into life where our feet earth touched. There was then none like us, who could love so much? Was it where we longed to be, wanting it so much.

.

Vipers slid round our feet, unseen to blind eyes. Venom works way deep inside, separates love-friends. Wailing with the question now is this how it ends.

Author notes

Interesting how family can at times be the most poisonous companions. They can and must be overcome.

In The Dead of Winter

In the dead of winter, in the coldest night, I have seen a wondrous thing. When life is gone and the Earth is still, I have seen SOME-THING. In the blackest night, in the depths of death, I have seen a miracle. In burning rock and seething cold, we see LIFE Again.

In deep December, when all is still, and trees are stripped of leaves. When all is lost, I wander out to see just what I will. There at the end of branches dead, a sight makes my heart sing. There at the end of branches dead I find the buds of Spring.

So God has given Life her Head, and a power that will not stop. Through hell and water, freeze, and drought, we will see Life Again. Yes, She is strong and will not stop, She always finds a way. Stand up my child, wake up and walk, take hold of Life Today.

Author notes

Inspired by working in our yard one winter

I am Alive

I am here, I am alive
I have been made strong through the fire, I will prevail.
I climb mountains, I cross raging rivers, because they are there and there is no other way.

What choice do I have but to climb, cross and prevail? I am here, I am alive and I prevail because I am alive and that is what it means to be alive.

There is no choice, no other way, no option but to do what I must in this life, and so.. I am here, I am alive
I have been made strong through the fire, through the pain, but I will prevail.

I climb mountains, I cross raging rivers, because they are there... What else can I do??? I cannot give up, I cannot surrender, I cannot turn away.

Because.....I am alive.

and that is what it means to be alive

Author notes

Rather than coming from an opinion that I have Arrived or that I am Superior or a Great Man. I write this from the perspective of one that has been through the fire and the flood and is still standing. That's not because of great endurance but from the view that we have no choice but to go through what we must go through in this life. It is all too often painful and grinding but we have no choice but to push through to the other side, no matter what and we must do that because we are alive.

Soon Enough

Soon enough comes the dark horse to ride me again
A cold stone for my heart, and for my mind, dread
Spurs sharpened on my teeth, pain now add to all my grief
Trample me now my soul black and blue
As I look to the sky and wait on You

Author notes

Written during a rather bad time in my life. The start of a journey of self-discovery and recovery whose start was very painful. That's when I started writing. Hmmm

We Begin Again

The fog is pierced from inside out
As we begin again
Clinging vines snagged all about
But, we begin again
Crashed the wall at 80 plus

See, we begin again
Thrust through shot through, cannot fight through
Still, we begin again
Once and forever, forever and again
We begin again
Matters not what happens friend
We begin again...

Author notes

Never stop, never quit...

Angles In Route

Ring, ringing alarm inside my skull
Up Son, Up, Go up
Stat! Up Son, fly now...
On Mercury's wings I fly
Hero's landing, place of dread

Face down, placid ghoul
What, what have you done
Why, where have you gone
Face down, alphabet face, drooling

Racing heart, no air. Direction.
Up, down to the floor, arms stiff
Just like...
What? Yes, I know, yes, I can...
Yes, I will, Stop The Reaper
Angles in route

My God!! PUSH, PUSH!!!
INTO THE DEAD PUSH LIFE!
Beyond soul death
Rapier in Legion Pierce me

Angels in route
Push, swoosh, push

Real, no TV, no Movie
Push
I am dying

Angles alight
We are here
She is ours
Task is ours

You are here, breathe the air
Angels fly, with you
I, sit, and stare
Breathe the air

Author notes

I was in the house working downstairs when an unknown panic struck me. I ran upstairs to find my wife unconscious and not breathing her face on the keyboard. I called 911 and at their direction started CPR successfully It's not like TV or as you see in the movies and with a loved one, parts of you die in the process... You'll never be the same, never.

FAITH

Crystal Columns

.

Flee from battle raging far behind, our forces crushed to dust. Filled with fear, ran from there, all was in despair.

.

Bridge of crossing, safety there far on the other side. Make it there breath the air, leave defeat behind.

.

Broken, shattered desperate bridge, crossing heart in hand. A mile or more it was to cross, reaching safety's hand. Still, we made it there at last, into that safe land.

.

Forces drove hard to the front, ours a force no more. Carry on the battle, as we leave the front. We will need a day and days, must erase our want.

.

Walking through a wedding field, all dressed, in fine pomp, the glory of their personhood, my God, I Know them all. Not in this fine glory here, but friends one and all.

.

One dressed in Glory comes, with coffee of celestial bliss. Dancing singing, joyous for me, though of me, He knows all. Knows me then, knows me now and before the fall.

.

As he leaves, I hear his soul cry, Welcome To Your House.

.

He goes left, I to the right, through grand portal inside. Then the glory of it all near destroyed my eyes. Tis a place no man deserves all gold, crystal, bronze. Columns of pure crystal abound, but what's this in them bound.

.

Gazing fixed inside this one, breath catches with a sigh. There, bound in Crystal, memories of She and We and I. Those things done for The King as decades passed by.

.

There I see a railing, again purest crystal, gold. Right, winding walkway flows down to golden silken pool. I thought, Shield-Maiden must see this, yes she must see it all, and see The One that knew me, us, before The Fall.

Author notes

This is a very long poem for me. It's a reflection of a long-detailed dream I had years ago. This dream greatly impacted me, and I've remembered it always. In documenting the dream in Poetry, I'm brought closer to the reality that during the dream the bridge I'm crossing isn't just a bridge and that the other side really is The Other Side

No End To His Kingdom

There is no end to His Kingdom, it's increase beyond Light Speed. Not just in song and verse but in truth indeed. Cosmic Event Horizon, as far as we can see, but Out There galaxies ignore Light Speed. Not bad speedin, just Light Speed they ignore, gotta make room, His Kingdoms busting out the doors...

All Will Be New

Think not of Them as you seek Me.
Many still broken, cracks in them, even yours I see. They are not Me, it is, I AM you should seek... Remember The Disciples, that foolish lot, I worked on them till all was Pure, not one blot.

.

In the Old Word, I admonished My People, stiff necked, prideful, sinful, still.. My People.

.

Now hatred flows from My Church, forgotten from them, the Love of My Words, My Work.

.

Still...

.

My Fire will purge them, them and yes you. Dross will be cleared, like Gold all is new. Then, My son, Little One you will see, My Finished work in them, My Work in thee. All will know, that I AM, AND, WILL ALWAYS BE.

How Many Times?

How many bullets will I dodge? I know nothing in all, only in part.
How many symptoms will the scans displace?
How many times I've looked death on the face...
How many times I should have been taken...
How many times will I find I'm not forsaken?
How many times have I jumped off that place, only to land in His love and grace...

Author notes

My life's journey has had many hairpin turns and narrow escapes...

Easter Morning

We live in desperate times, on this glorious Easter Morning.

.

Death lurkers all around, hear Christ's Resurrection story.

.

So many have, will die, and be seated at His Table, remember this, that, in all things He is able.

.

Verily, Verily I say to you, you will have tribulations, through your tears, Keep your head up, look to Me, I am able

.

When all seated at the promised Christ Reunion table. All together sing His praise, we live forever because He is able...

.

What Will You Do...

Ahhh You are righteous, just and true, in my soul I admit it.

.

King of all glory, whom justice will do, and once again I admit it.

.

The One who was and is to come, King of all glory is You.

.

Oh, I can hear you whisper to me, my child what will you do...

Author notes

This one just exploded in my mind...

I am...

My heart beats and in this, I AM
Think not foolishly, I Am not HIM
BUT, I am
I am His child, a Little One in His Power
Thus I Am...
My heart breaks, filled with joy and indeed, I am
My path is straight, I lose my way and again, I am
Shield-Maiden reaches out in love, and with Joy, I am
The Star Queen on her throne, it's pillars, my heart's creation
Thus here again, I am
Been through The Test, The Long Dark Night, been close to death

But, but, here, I live and indeed, I am
Life full of Good, Horrors of the night
His Light shining bright
I am...

Author notes

I have to think about what to say about this one...

In Heaven thar ain't no Restin in Peace .

No, I ain't done, it ain't all been spend of what Heaven done sent

.

I still got Life and it should suffice to get me where I'm meant to get

.

Ain't no time to rest, you're Heaven Blessed, we don't go to Heaven to Rest

.

There'll be chores to do, corral a Star or two, make sure them Pulsars well kept.

.

You'll git to Roll Your Own, Wormholes strait like a bone. Go on, Roll em and quit

.

Make sure Super-Novas splode on time, you do yours, I'll do mine

.

Just makin sure you know, Rest in Peace is a crime. In Heaven, ya'll don't lie supine.

.

Author notes; Now where the heck did that come from??

Conversation without the politics of Poo

We spoke for some time these Brothers and I bound by a Merry Christmas. No social commentaries, it had no place in conversation of God's Grace.

.

We spoke of what is seen out there, His Creation beyond our air. Grandure, glory, beyond compare. How we, small and simple think we're so fair.

.

Stars a thousand times Sol's size, make Sol seem dime-sized. Twas all about Him, and Him born-crucified Amazing Grace come to open our eyes.

.

Astrophysics chasing God, but they don't know why. We spoke of discoveries, Up and Down Quarks and those Strange and Charmed Quarks too. Giving glory for what He had done and what He will do.

.

To speak with those Brothers of His Might and Power without the politics of Poo, now this conversation uplifted the soul and gave the mind food.

Author notes

A nice uplifting conversation on Christmas day...

Christmas, know who He was..

Christmas is an empty song without Easter's refrain. Without Easter, my friends, nothing could remain.

.

Without Easter can't you see, HE may have destroyed all. The final resolution, Death, to Man's sinful fall.

.

From eternity past He knew Christ death would save us all. That saving could not have been done if in Heaven He did stall.

.

Think a moment, no stop and think who He was as Lord of all. In eternity past all creation quaked at Jesus Christ foot falls.

.

Angels and Archangels, who made men faint and fall, laid face down, souls prostrate at Jesus Christ call.

.

Those twinkly, shining starry things some thousands times the size of Sol, Jesus Christ made every one, by name He knows them all.

.

Shhh, there is now more being made, His Glory has no walls.

.

Quasar-Pulsar is His pet, Gamma-Ray Burst His call. Know now friends this is The One who came at Christmas to save us all.

Author notes

Christmas takes on a whole new meaning when we realize just who Christ was and is..

And Yet

Shadowlands
Through Shadowlands we walk
No, no, we grapple
Grapple, brawl, indeed we fight
Thick molasses, neck deep, push, push, push
Breathe, surge, breathe, move forward

Fallen cosmos, the enemy
Prince of The Air, God Damns you, I curse you,
Cosmic Gettysburg long ago passed, and yet...
Glory and Gore prevailed to freedom, end of story known and yet..
Birth to death, fight, contend, victory, defeat, to the end, finally
Open eyes, to see Him... At Last..

Christ's Door

Death, the final enemy, strikes again and again. Sons and Daughters of God wailing "When Lord When" as death strikes again, and again.

.

Ten thousand years, we've walked the Earth and Always, Always, We Die. Some believe death is the end, but that's just a lie.

.

All ancients knew death was no end, our eternal spirits knew why. At the death of death stands The King, arms still open wide.

.

There with Him are multitudes, those we knew had gone before. Feel the love of their embrace as you walk through Christ Door..

Author notes

The Death of death is coming.

Beyond Pax Romana

Ahh, this is not IT, to live, grow, fly then die. Die, in pain smothered. No this is not it. No tis not.

.

Every village Chief, Priest and fool knows eternal is our soul. Lives in shadowlands awaits release of the soul.

.

Feet mired in temporal mud sucking up to the knee. No, in shadowlands we are, but we should not be.

.

Human spirits screaming for release, answered by His eternal Peace. Then beyond Pax Romana will we be.

.

Till then, know the temporal will not always be....

Author notes

Amazing how all living things die, but we (humans) have always known that we are Eternal in our true nature

Box Too Small

He is not in a box to think and act as we do. Nor His ways ours, or His thoughts so small, so human.
.

As the ocean sits neatly in a thimble, so His thoughts in our heads. As Betelgeuse rests upon human hand, so His ways into ours.
.

As leviathan is our pet, so He at our Beck and call. Remember, Little One, Dear Little One, He is Lord of All.

Author notes

Creator in contrast to the created ones. He does not have to do anything the way that we think it should be done or must have been done.

Ancients Knew

Look, Orion in the sky, know the ancients knew it Christ. Bruised heel crush the serpents head, club swung down in might. King of all suffered pain in battle, breaks the chains of death. See His glory across the sky, as you take each breath.

Author notes

I've loved the constellation Orion. As it rises each winter, I'm reminded of God's watching over me. There are other interpretations of the constellations, other than the Greek and Roman descriptions.

What He Has Done

I have seen the glory of His creation and am undone. Though tis, a shadow of glory yet to come. Walk in reverence, look, above. Tremble in fear, then know His Love.

.

We cannot fathom what He has done. So simple for Him, the creation of suns. Where were we when Sons of God sang. When all that is from His power sprang.

SOCIAL

No End

His creation has no end
His glory knows no boundaries
His kingdom's everlasting growth
Sings Creation's story
Not, as we understand but more
Universe, Multiverse unending
A sea of glass endlessly stretched
So to the increase of His kingdom

Author notes

His Kingdom is indeed everlasting and looking around I'm
glad of it

Till Shiloh Come

There will be no peace till Shiloh come, of all things this is true
He will set aside our fears, our wars, our hates our feuds

There will be no peace till Shiloh come, no matter what the
cause
Claim it for this, claim it for that, fact is, we're all lost

There will be no peace till Shiloh come, the fix is in no pill
We spill blood, we spill milk, fact is, we're all ill

There will be no peace till Shiloh come, so hasten on the day
He will set aside our death, death was the price He paid

Author notes

As we observe the world, we see a world of hurt. There is glory
in our world but so much pain and evil also. Shiloh is term
used as a foreshadowing mention of Christ.

"The scepter shall not depart from Judah, nor a lawgiver from
between his feet, until Shiloh comes, and unto him shall the
gathering of the people be." (Genesis 49:10)

Pearls of Mountians

Pearls of mountains, strung out over time
Points of power, points of might
Places of majesty
Pushed up from the depths of the earth
A power subject to the Almighty Places of greatness.

Snow white crystal flowing down, down, down
To the valleys below, draped in darkness
Giving life, giving breath, giving hope
Heat giving birth to cold
Cold giving life and warmth
Life from the Father Warmth from the Son

Let your Spirit flow down to us, Oh Most High
Spirit giving life to flesh
Flesh giving place to Spirit
Your Love giving life to all Reversing the curse
Reversing the fall.

Author notes

I've done a lot of writing while flying around the country on business. This was written while flying over the Cascade Mountains.

Rivers of Air

There are rivers of air,
up there
Strong moving air,
up there
They push and pull,
up there
Strong rippling air,
up there
Here them roar,
up there
Through clouds they channel,
up there
Making hills and valleys,
up there
Opening windows,
up there
To let the Son in, down there

Author notes

This was written while flying on business. Somehow flying and seeing the world below inspires me.

Across The Void

Reach across the void, and know they are there. Cross the desert of despair to find them. Heart and soul, strong enough to bridge the great divide.

.

They now, know and soon will we the reason of Christ "Why". At His Great Table, multitudes abide with those we lost, no simple By and By but side by side.

Author notes

Two deaths in our family in the last couple of months, one of which was Very Unexpected. My First Cousin died within an hour of my Aunt's burial

Three Days

Roaring as they watched His pain
Triumphant as He suffered
Laughing as each drop of blood
Fell carrying our suffrage
Enraptured beyond all joy
Seeing Son Set glory fading
Three days they did dance and sing
We've put him in the grave now
When the celebrations done
We'll topple heavens towers
Once archangels are destroyed
Mankind we'll devour
.

Supernova power surged
Riding Gama-Ray-Burst power
Shaming the glory of Big Bang
Thundering Salvation's hour
Word of Life surged from the grave
Trampling deaths power
.

Dragging legions off in chains
Gifts given to His children
This was Gettysburg's last day
In the cosmic story

We'll fight on for a day and days
Knowing the end of the story
In His power and His might
We now seek His glory

Notes:

Thankful for the most important event in the history of the Cosmos.

You May Suffer, You will Suffer

Verily, I say to you
You may suffer
You will suffer
Remember, all my words are true
You may suffer
You will suffer
Cosmic Gettysburg has passed
You may suffer
You will suffer
I am The First and The Last
You may suffer
You will suffer
It's for a short, short time
That You may suffer
That You will suffer

I will come for you in time
Reclaim you, you are Mine
Lift you to the heights
Exalt you in my Might
Show you the work you've done
How you served The Son
When you suffered
Though you suffered

Author notes

As time passes, I find that we must face this fact; that most of us will suffer and some will suffer terribly. We have assurance from Above, but it's a bitter pill to swallow...

His Children

I am of Christ
My Shieldmaiden is of Christ
Look, gaze upon these wounds
Scars, terrible
The work of His children
God's Children
How can this be
How Can This Be
God is love
The Enemy laughs
We must wait
The time to victory will pass

Latter Rain

Slamin, slamin, slamin, slamin
Oh, God how it hurts
I'm lifted up, thrown to the ground
My face is filled with dirt
I'm getting stronger, yes, I am
But now I feel the pain
I'm looking up into the sky
Waiting for Latter Rain

Author notes

Life is at times an Interesting and Complex journey

The First and the Last

His face hidden in the mountain
While The Lord God passed by
Proclaiming His Glory
That He would never die
Here before the beginning
Alive past the end of time
Grace, power, glory
In Him abide
He did not stop
Nor return to His abode
Till He had died, to save human souls

Face set like a lion
He set to the task
He died and He rose
The first and the last

Author notes

Almost all that we need to know about God is in His expression
of Himself to Moses in Exodus 34:6-7.

Quiet Time

In the quiet time my mind goes out, seeking the start of all things. Breaking these bonds of mine, let my mind unwind, let it go wandering 5000, 10000 one million years back, stand at the portals of time
Now wonders my mind, what will I find good god, I've come so far. I watch Him arise, The Lord of all time, He who was and is to come
Falling to knees, in tears I plead as my sins have chased me through time And as I plead, He touches me saying, Beloved, Come

Author notes

As King David said, wherever I go Lord, you are there...

He made us, from the stuff of stars...

He made us, from the stuff of stars
His love demands we not stay as we are
He has named us as His friends
How can we offend again and again
He's ascribed eternity in our souls
Yet we seek to die, alone and cold
Few wonder how this can be
Having plucked out our eyes
We cannot see...

Author notes

We are made so wonderfully, yet at times we sink so low..

Blue Marble

To gaze upon the night sky is to see glory
Absolute glory, frightening glory
Shatters our pride
beyond us, above us, surpassing us
we, on our blue marble
Small, blue marble
insignificant, invisible
Still, He sees us

Author notes Sadly, we make mountains of such small things
as we live on this tiny blue marble hung is space. In perspective
it's amazing that He sees us at all, yet He does and loves us in
spite of our smallness and insanity.

Look up

My God, my God
Why have you loved me
One so small, so prone to sin
I am filled with nothing within

Screams of the accuser I hear again
Thou hast done thus and thus
In hell I will grind your bones to dust

Hear the cry of archangels child look up
See The One in whom you trust
Riding the winds He comes at last
The King of Glory, the first and last
He did not wait to save your soul
Crushing the enemy fore any sun rose

Shout His praise
Turn from the past
Hold faith in The First, and The Last

Author notes

He's always there... Found this in my Drafts folder... Don't remember writing it..

American Deeds

Watch, as I kill my children
Both born and unborn
Demons of Rights and Desires
I leave not forlorn
Feed them children's blood
Gnaw sinew and bone
I scream and cry at each death
But God knows I'm not done
For my rights of this and that
I slay both night and day
Out Damn spot, oh do wash out
The blood is here to stay
Fact is I don't give a Damn
Long as I get my way

Author notes

Will Americans continue to kill their (our) children? Politicians with their Thoughts and Prayers. God, please save us from ourselves.

Wet Market Games.

Aaahhhh, I can't breathe!! A few more steps, I'll be free... Out into open air, rip accursed mask off, surge air.

.

Damn, how did this happen? Wet Market games? Damn those Wet Markets, savagery, cruelty, shame.

.

Yes we know all must eat, open eyes now see crimes. Human lives, now the cost of Wet Markets grime.

.

No, not just Over There, do we see this game. The world over humans play extermination games.

.

A Thousand ways we create to die, not just one but all. Perhaps we are, like them building Fermi's wall.

.

Fermi Paradox solution not so hard at all. Perhaps they just like us, built their wall, built it just to fall. They built their wall just to fall, and how great was that fall...

.

We stand atop Fermi's wall. Perhaps we'll jump, perhaps we'll fall...

.

Perhaps we don't deserve to be here at all...

Author notes

Are we Killing Ourselves off??

Christophany of Christ

Joshua, mighty man of God, in the morn trod his battle line.

Came upon a Mighty Man sword drawn, strong as mountain standing on the other side. Said Joshua, the mighty man of God, are you with us, or against?

Joshua knew deep in his heart that God his side did bless..

No, rather I indeed come now as captain of the host of the Lord, Christophany replied. Crushing lesson here to learn is Christ is on God's side.

Far left and right scream day and night God's ALL IN FOR US!!! In God's eyes, we're all the same, ashes to ashes, dust to dust. How is it, we Little Ones forgot, in ourselves, we cannot trust... Peel back the thin veneer, come, see our Blood Lust...

Author notes

Oh so proudly flawed we are..

Now when Joshua was near Jericho, he looked up and saw a man standing in front of him with a drawn sword in his hand. Joshua went up to him and asked, "Are you for us or for our enemies?"

.

14"Neither," he replied, "but as commander of the army of the Lord I have now come." Then Joshua fell facedown to the ground in reverence, and asked him, "What message does my Lord have for His servant?"

.

15The commander of the Lord's army replied, "Take off your sandals, for the place where you are standing is holy." And Joshua did so.

Off Sides!!

I love my side, as they are of my side, as such, hate those of that side, as They are that side. Believe I my side as they are my side, it follows, lies only on that side, not my side, not my side. On my side god abides, not that side of lies. It follows that, that side of lies must die and my side abides at god's side, now that's no lie... Glory to my side...

What!! I can't hear you, you're on the wrong side...so am I...

Thought Upon Thought.

Suppression of thought brings national death, as does thinking only Our way is best. Swallow thought without thought and thus fail the test. Those that hate free thought give us no rest, not knowing static thought is not blessed. I dig what CIA, NSA say. Who said that, why, and should we think that way? All and all, and at the end of the day, we've all believed enough lies for one day. We've all swallowed enough poop, let's sit down, think, reflect on the front stoop.

Author notes

Let's all take a mental Break...

Choose Not to Believe (it matters not)

Screaming as they die, it's not real!! Steel blade inside me.. a phantom
Fluid-filled lungs, a nothing, they say I'll die, that's just bluffing.
Who's that I hear huff-puffing?
.

O2 now below 60. None of your lies be fitting.
I lie not prone, but sit sipping, sipping on lies, skinny dipping.
Living The Life, that's My Right. Struggle against all, cause, I'm Right...
.

Now no need to breathe, from the ceiling looking down to see, and oh my what I see. I was wrong, times run out for me.

Author notes

Objective Truth does not care what we believe or think...

What It's All About

Smacked in the face, the desperate think tomorrow will not
come. yes, my friends, it does, it does and then again does.
.

The disciples thought it's over now, they've laid Him in the
grave. How is it that they forgot that from the grave He'd be
raised
A foolish man killed a cop, screamed study Revelations. Poor
wretched man had studied not, now to his damnation.
.

Perhaps we should leave Christmas out, with little celebration.
Easter's what it's all about, Christ death to save all Nations.
.

Author notes

You know What It's All About...

Write, Right

Right, write as to write is right
To write is right as life is right
Of this and that, and that to write
If a fight, then write of what is right
Of that, and this, this and that do write
To do right is to write of right
To write, not fist fight is right
Write of right, to preserve life, is right

.

Author notes

As always, just do what's right..

On The 6th

I heard them cry out on the 6th, Adams and Jefferson wailing

.

Their graves, North and South disrupted again, as they spun arms flailing

.

In anger they spin, once and again, American Experiment failing

.

Stop, read their words, their letters explaining, experiments foundation's leading

.

Set aside hate, now, please don't wait, move forward, love prevailing

Thankful

Time to be Thankful in this time of strife.
Look to His Power, His Grace, His Might.
Live or die, it will be alright..Live or die, all in His sight.
Time to be Thankful for all you have.
That One beside you, joyful or sad.
Watch your generations move forward in time.
Rejoice for the Mountains you did climb.
For what you have lost, yet you are still here.
For those brave times and those filled with fear.
In sickness and in health, stretches you far.
Till death does us part, unites those near and far.
Be Thankful, My Friends that you still are.....
Live or die, it will be alright. Live or die, all in His sight

Fields Of The Dead

I arise again, you do not what you should
Fools, know who I am, what I will do
These, I slay, drown them inside
Some I ignore, still you should hide
The young, some I main, Kawasaki you know not why

.

Please take your Rights, yes, help me spread
Cures from Laymen, Fools, You Should Dread
I'm changing inside, I see fields of the dead

Author notes

More and More die every day...

Writing and Writing and Writing...

Writing and writing, writing, and writing about writing and this and that over there. Writing and writing and writing, and writing, about seeing the path oh so clear. Writing and writing and writing, and writing about not seeing the path very clear. Writing and writing and writing and writing about stopping and breathing to let my mind clear. Writing and writing and writing, and writing about thinking more clearly and deeply out here...

Author notes

Ever get carried away with Writing??

CANCER

I Am Afraid (there, I said it..)

Read, read your poems son
Read and remember
Seek, speak truth of yourself
Your words

.

I'm ok, it's nothing, I'm fine

.

Foolishness, child's lies to self
Suffering, yes suffering, is truth
Your truth

.

It's matters of degree so...

.

Be still child, know, remember
Pain, suffering
Not like others of Lejeune, still..
Suffering is so and in you

.

Itch, yes now that
Infection, on and on
Your words?

.

Alligator Skin Cracks open, oh God not again. Six, nine
months, not again, not again, not again.

.

I am afraid...

.

Yes, now child
Now in confession, are you ready..
Take up shield and sword and light
Your Shield-Maiden on your right
Face forward and back into the fight

Author notes

This is a rather disrespectful conversation with myself in poetry (strange format). I think that in all my Pumping myself up to fight cancer, perhaps I've neglected to acknowledge and address my Fear. It good and best to fight, but without fear, there is no courage. In my poetry, I speak often of my pain, but I think I forget that and move on too easily. The issue is that I've been fighting a chemo related infection for over six months now... Damn..

Tonight, I sink down, for this night, one night...

Tonight, I sink down, for this night, one night.

.

Cancer is in flight, tamed, chained. Chemo saves yet, causes ill...

.

Tamed cancer, stalled immune system, infection fills the gap.

.

Tamed infection, but, but it comes back. Once, twice and again

.

Alligator skin, cracks open, good God not again... In the Gulfstream I need to swim. Salt healing waters from back then

.

Nephrologist says that part of you's destroyed, but this pill will renew that joy.

.

Yes, tonight I sink down. Tomorrow's fight, to retake lost ground

.

Shield-maiden brightened today. Come now son, get back in the game.

Author notes

Funny, it's not (for me) usually not the cancer but the chemo related issues. Today, rather sucked with all that but tomorrow is another day...

Side Effects of Side Effects

Another one

Side Effects of Side Effects, drugs upon drugs. Oh, how I curse those that brought this flood. Know, some now so wealthy, so very well off, Bastards poisoned us, then simply ran off. 40 years of crimes, but no ones in jail Camp LeJeune Families cry, die and wail. One Million Plus face LeJeune's blade but, we'll show them of what we're made...

Author notes; Just dealing with yet another side effect of the chemo treatment I'm on for CLL. Can't and won't stay down long but we have to be honest about how we feel yes?

Silly Pill

Another pill to stay alive, yes take them day by day. Not one alone, no not just one, a cohort swilled each day. I hate to down them day by day, but to stay alives my drive. So come now thou silly pill, I'll eat you now alive.

Author notes

Funny thought about the many pills/meds I take related to chemo for Leukemia. I'm fine and will continue to be as it's very well controlled.

Unkind Words For Cancer

You knew who I was, so why come for me. I'm a Viking, a Saint, I Will Not Flee.
Peer into my heart, see the fire inside me. Remember my Father, Combat V? Like him I will fight and no, I'll not quit. So, come on damn you, I'll toss your ass in the ditch.

Author notes

Fight, Cancer at all costs

Side Effects

Pills
So many
The hard ones
Break in two
Swallow whole
I cannot
Three chemo, soft
Easy
Seven for chemo pain.. HA!!
2 AM, Chemo surgeons arise
Slice into shoulder

Bisect the biceps
Flay open the forearm
Drill into wrist
Oh, did that wake you?
Apologies..
Done in a few
There now, all done (for tonight)
Tomorrow then..??
F.U.
Fine see you then
Clock ticks close to 9PM
Feel the ache
Take the pills
They will be here soon
Listen to Dad's voice
This will not kill you
You can take it
You can take it
You can take it

Author notes

Chronic Lymphocytic leukemia is an interesting part if my life. All things being equal I will die with it but not from it. CLL would be a non-issue except that I take a very effective chemotherapy (Imbruvica) with it's side Effects of Musculoskeletal Pain which sucks rather badly... Still, in those dark times (always at night), I can hear my Father's voice.

Screaming Nightmare

Asleep, dreaming, nothing
Shot in the arm
Pain, deep pain
In the muscle, the bone
Bolt upright, nothing
Scream, nothing

Do anything, nothing
Fear, I am afraid
Fear's friend, hyperventilation
Screaming, thrashing, nothing
Nothing
Shieldmaiden is near, but
Nothing
Trusted help, but nothing
hyperventilating, roaring fear, terror
Nothing
Finally, faintly, the voice
Voice of battles fought, won
The voice of battles, lost, survived
Growing stronger, closer
Peace, calm
Be peace, be calm
Be, Awake, and I am
Nightmare, fleeing
Galloping away
I am awake
What the hell???

Author notes

This nightmare and today's attacks of chemo induced musculoskeletal pain pushed me over the edge for the first time (I've had CLL for 7 years). I woke up in pain and confused so I wrote about it. Had a great business meeting this morning, then another massive attack. I must learn something from this. I will be strong again tomorrow, for now my Shieldmaiden is with me and I take comfort in that.

I Stand

I am here
Here I stand
Your blows strike home
Vicious as a sworn enemy
Crippled with pain
Dreading the next attacks
But
I am here and I am at war
Cannot, will not give in
Not in my nature

Come ahead
Attack
Here I stand and always will
Born, bred, trained among Battle Fields
Battlefield Districts

So come
I will fight without end
And in the end
I will stand

Author notes

Life throws all manner of deep dark tainted mojo at us. For me it's CLL. Pray, fight, get knocked down but Good Gravy, get back up...

With Cancer

With cancer
Life is
What's that
Or that
Am I fine
I don't know

I'm not in danger
I know, I think
I am
With cancer

Author notes

Cancer changes everything. Every change in your body is suspect. You're always wondering what's next. Things are going well, but are they?

Tree of Life

Sit beside the tree
Supposed tree of life
Blood concoction flows to me
Keeping me alive
Designed for me
Only for me
My Army, crossing the sea
Living to kill, what would kill me
Victory is mine, Damn you, You'll see...

Author notes

This is a reflection of my first round of chemo infusion. While that round of chemo failed, I always knew that I would prevail in the end. As much as possible, fight like hell whatever is dumped in your path.

Chemo Round Two

I swore to slay you, and I did
Now, I return
To Slay those that you hid

Author notes

In my first round of chemo, I told my CLL that I would attack it with all military power at my disposal and that later, I would return to destroy its descendants.

Back Again

Back again?
Well, may you be damned
I am not God, but He made me as I am
One that will fight, will never quit
Born, raised in Battlefield Districts
Like them, I will fight
Till I have won
Remember, damn you
I'm my Father's son

Author notes

Woke up with some chemo pain a bit ago, so well, I wrote about it. My Father fought his cancers with courage born amidst the Carnage of Vietnam. In both cases, he fought like a Tiger and was without fear...

Still Around?

So, you're still around...
My goal is to beat you, beat you down
In battle with you, I'll not quit
Feel forever the wrath of my fist
With heart and soul, I war with you...
Know that in the end.. I'll kill you...
With Agent Orange, you took my Father
The poison of LeJeune's water
Know this now and forever more
With you, I Am At WAR...

Author notes; This is the only way that I can feel about the cancers that my Father got from chemical exposure while serving our country and the CLL, I had from drinking poisoned water at Camp LeJeune Marine Corp Base. Seems my Father's Fighting Spirit lives in me...

WAR

A Young Man Went off to War

A young man went off to war
My God, what did you see
In the Operating Room
On the field of battle
See the young men suffer
Watch them bleed
Crying out in pain
Their young lives draining away
Dying as you fought to save them
Slipping away, through your hands into death
Death, pain, suffering
Till you had the look
Hollowed out, having seen too much
Finite vessel filled with infinite grief
Leaking out till death did you part
Oh my Father
You were a young man, that went off to war
Someone else came back
In the field
How many did you save
Wretching life back from death
Staunch the bleeding
Push life's breath back in
Look up, see another one down
Then up and off at a run again
No thought of yourself
Save them, save them save
Fight and save, you're now
Combat V, Combat V, means nothing now
You're broken, broken, broken

Dead inside
War survivor, broken man came home
A young man with off to war
Someone else came back

Your reward
The agent named Orange ravaged you
LeJeune H2O, poisoned you
Took your life, though war could not
Victories in combat, eclipsed by death
A young man went off to war
Someone else came back
We all suffered

.

.Chuck Worthy
Gig Harbor WA 04/22/2018

Author notes

Like many, my Father went to war in Viet Nam. This is another tribute to his bravery and the price he paid. A Young Man went Off To War, someone else came back. The Combat V designation is for sustained valorous conduct in battle under fire. How fitting for My Father.

Should Not Have Been...

Awaken in the middle of the night, reaching for one not there. Taken by sniper unseen, my god, it's obscene. Young perfect man serving a nation's plan, killed, the reason unseen and again tis obscene. Cash flows freely to the unseemly, used by them to kill uncleanly, so unclean, his death should not have been. When will we learn that always is not when?

Author notes

Count the cost before going to war. Make sure it's a worthy cause and worth the price

Danny Grimes

Danny Grimes spent his time in The 13th Valley Grinder.

A Young Man went, someone else came back, a shameful nation broke its Pact.
.

Broke it's Pact, spit on him when he came back, having earned valor and honor.
.

He, They, gave glorious sacrifice; the nation repaid shame. Fought like a Tiger, for the Brothers he loved. Gave his youth for the nation.
.

Young Men go to war, old men come back. Youth dies, don't you know, in the first attack.
.

He, They fought and never lost, no not one major Battle. Men of The Hill, some climbing still, Battle-Scarred in battle...
.

Now count the cost of war, come, look into the matter. Counting up the horrid cost, add Family, Niece, and Brother.

Author notes

My wife and I were having a business conversation with a woman and somehow the conversation turned to our families and how they had been affected by a Loved One's service in Vietnam. It's decades later but the families of Vietnam vets still suffer from the war's ever lasting pain flowing through generations.

Men of The Hill

My Father's Kin, his siblings still. American Combat Veterans,
Men of The Hill.
.

Shock, trauma they know. Up the hill to fight, souls restless not
still. Some won't make it... God's will?
.

Time dilation, wars setting still, into the fray, kind souls must
kill
.

Fight, kill, pieces inside die. Decades later, from this can't hide.
.

Years later, lay awake still, is enemy here, looking to kill?
Where's my K-Bar, keep it close still.
Hear, See them screaming, dying still. Calm down Old Son,
take the pill.
.

Thanks for your service, makes them smile, feel ill, Hear, See
them screaming, dying still.

Author notes

Another exploration of Vietnam and how it changed my Father.

Guards of the Unknown One

Like Steel they stand to Guard him
Unbroken honor stands upon the rock
None trespass to disturb his peace
Those that would, with force stopped
Guards of unrelenting force
Strong as rivers in their course.

As mountains frame the valley
They are with him now
His name still yet unknown
Before his grave heads bow
.

Author notes

The Grave of the Unknown Soldier rest on Hallowed Ground. My Father's grave is not far from this spot. He rests in honor with his Brothers and Sisters in Arms. Among those that have given all for their country.

Sentinels Before The Wall

They dwell beneath his Tomb that His honor may last, as Cherubim stand before The First and The Last. These have heard The Call, Stand as Sentinels before the wall. For all time standing tall, with honor, one and all. Honor, Courage, Pride, for His sake, for all time.

Author notes

Inspired by the Gaurds at The Tomb of The Unknown Soldier.

Riches of War

Long ago, we sent them to war, glory for us to attain

.

We, old and rich sent them out, without a care for their pain

.

Our prayers and hopes we sent with them, though tis not worth a damn

.

What our cursed souls want at all cost, be the riches under the sand...

Author notes

War is unavoidable at times, but every war brings financial gain to some inspite of the pain suffered by many.

www.ingramcontent.com/pod-product-compliance
Lightning Source LLC
Chambersburg PA
CBHW051237120626
46547CB00013B/1683